7/16

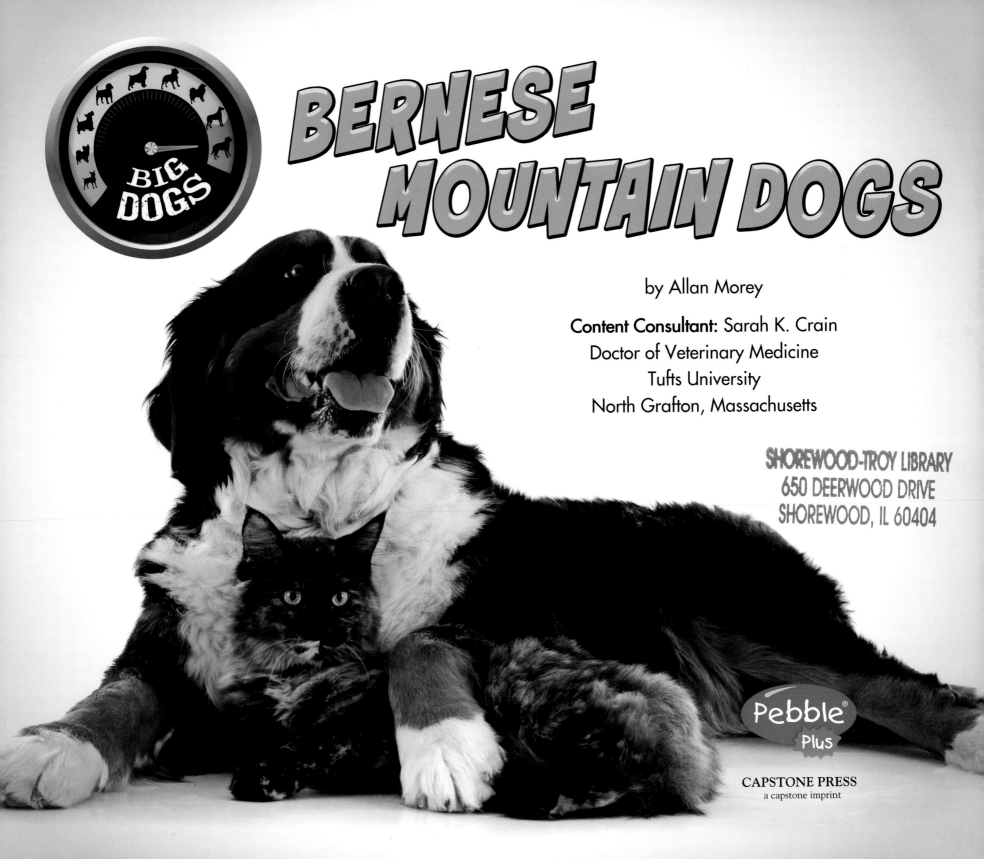

BIG DOGS

BERNESE MOUNTAIN DOGS

by Allan Morey

Content Consultant: Sarah K. Crain
Doctor of Veterinary Medicine
Tufts University
North Grafton, Massachusetts

Pebble® Plus

CAPSTONE PRESS
a capstone imprint

Pebble Plus is published by Capstone Press,
1710 Roe Crest Drive, North Mankato, Minnesota 56003
www.mycapstone.com

Library of Congress Cataloging-in-Publication Data
Names: Morey, Allan, author.
Title: Bernese mountain dogs / by Allan Morey.
Description: North Mankato, Minnesota : Capstone Press, a Capstone imprint,
   2016. | ?2016 | Series: Big dogs | Audience: Ages 5-7.? | Audience: K to
   grade 3.? | Includes bibliographical references and index.
Identifiers: LCCN 2015030283 | ISBN 9781491479827 (library binding)
Subjects: LCSH: Bernese mountain dog--Juvenile literature. | Dog
   breeds--Juvenile literature.
Classification: LCC SF429.B47 M67 2016 | DDC 636.73--dc23
LC record available at http://lccn.loc.gov/2015030283

Editorial Credits
Nikki Bruno Clapper, editor; Juliette Peters, designer;
Morgan Walters, media researcher; Katy LaVigne, production specialist

Photo Credits
Alamy: Juniors Bildarchiv GmbH, 15; Dreamstime: Winzworks, 9; Getty Images: Jill Lehmann
Photography, 21; Shutterstock: andrewvec, (speedometer) cover, Best dog photo, 7, cynoclub, 1,
Degtyaryov Andrey, 13, Eric Isselee, (dog) bottom left 22, Hywit Dimyadi, (dog silouette) cover,
kostolom3000, (dog head) backcover, 3, Mikkel Bigandt, (dog) cover, PHOTOCREO Michal
Bednarek, 17, rebeccaashworth, 19, Stephaniellen, (elephant) bottom right 22, vlastas, (paw prints)
design element throughout, Zuzule, 11; SuperStock: Juniors, 5

Note to Parents and Teachers

The Big Dogs set supports national science standards related to life science. This book describes and illustrates Bernese mountain dogs. The images support early readers in understanding the text. The repetition of words and phrases helps early readers learn new words. This book also introduces early readers to subject-specific vocabulary words, which are defined in the Glossary section. Early readers may need assistance to read some words and to use the Table of Contents, Glossary, Read More, Internet Sites, Critical Thinking Using the Common Core, and Index sections of the book.

Printed in the United States of America in North Mankato, Minnesota.
102015   009221CGS16

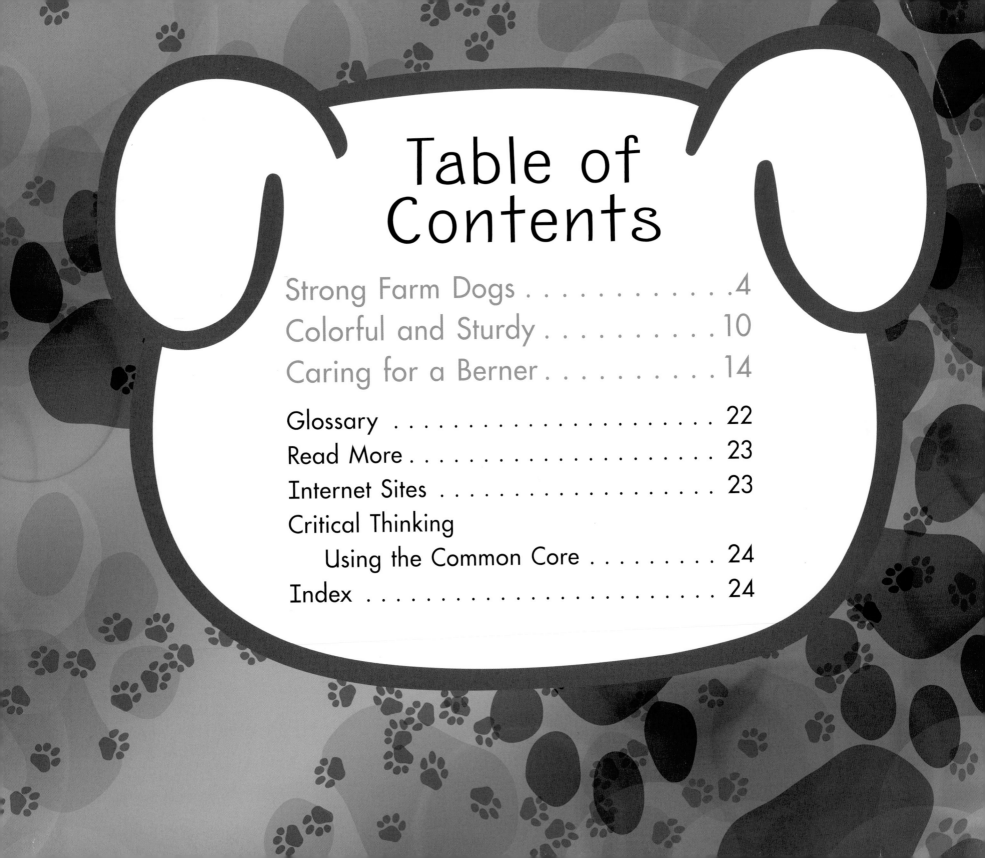

Table of Contents

STRONG FARM DOGS

Have you ever seen

a dog pull a heavy cart?

Big, strong Bernese

mountain dogs can do that.

Bernese mountain
dogs are working dogs.
They were bred to
herd livestock. They also
make good watchdogs.

You can call these dogs
Berners for short. Berners
are loyal to their families.
They are gentle with kids.

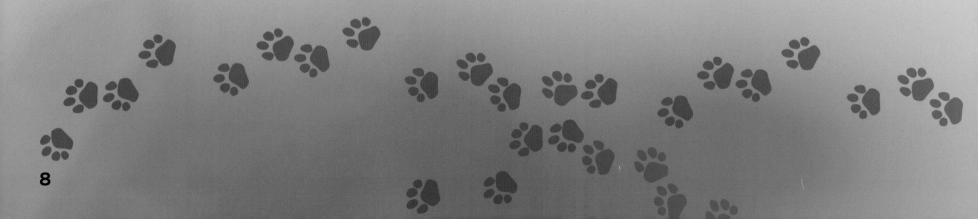

COLORFUL AND STURDY

Berners have thick

coats with three colors.

Most Berners are black

and white, plus tan

or rust.

The body of a Berner is sturdy and strong. These big dogs eat a lot. Food costs can add up quickly. Berners live for 7 to 8 years.

CARING FOR A BERNER

Berners can get protective around their families. They need to play with other pets and people.

Big dogs like Berners
must be well trained.
Owners get them used to
people and other dogs.

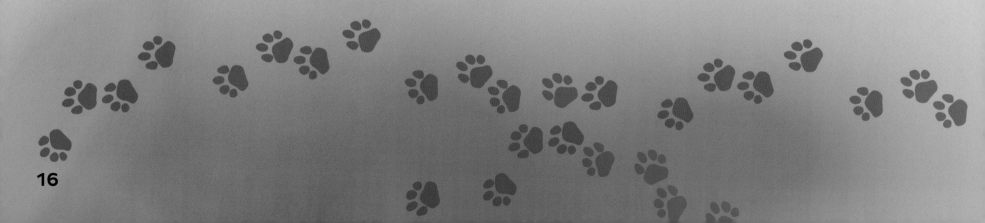

Do you like to walk
and play a lot? Berners do.
Exercise keeps them healthy
and well behaved.

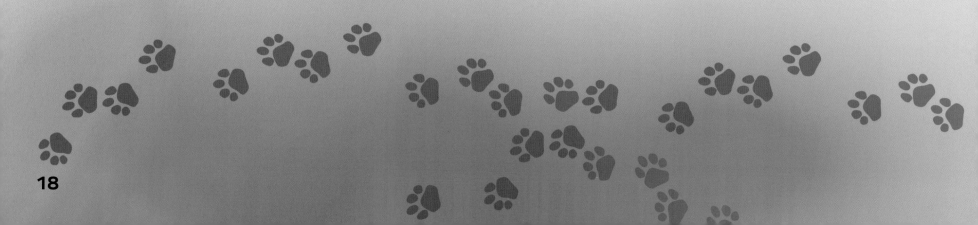

Bernese mountain dogs
are calm, friendly, and sweet.
They make great house pets.

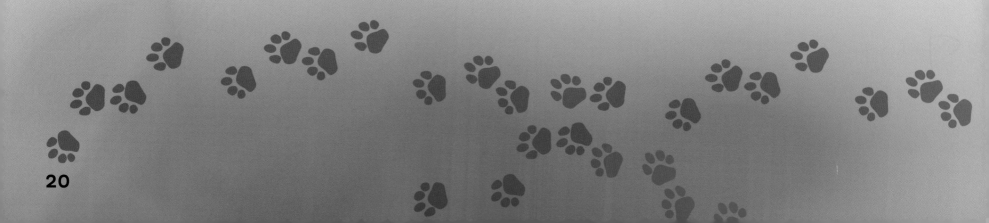

GLOSSARY

breed—to mate and produce young

coat—an animal's hair or fur

exercise—a physical activity done in order to stay healthy and fit

herd—to round up animals, such as cattle, and keep them together

livestock—animals raised on a farm, such as sheep and cows

loyal—being true to something or someone

protective—wanting to keep someone or something safe

watchdog—a dog trained to guard a house, property, or people

working dog—a dog that is bred to do a job, such as herding animals or guarding homes

HOW BIG ARE THEY?

Bernese Mountain Dog		Baby Elephant
Average Height	23–27 inches (58–69 centimeters)	36 inches (91 cm)
Average Weight	70–120 pounds (32–54 kilograms)	200 pounds (91 kg)

42
36
30
24
18
12
6
0

READ MORE

Meister, Cari. *Dogs.* My First Pet. Minneapolis, Minn.: Bullfrog Books, 2015.

Rustad, Martha E. H. *Dogs.* Smithsonian Little Explorer: Little Scientist. North Mankato, Minn.: Capstone Press, 2015.

Wheeler, Jill C. *Bernese Mountain Dogs.* Checkerboard Animal Library: Dogs. Edina, Minn.: ABDO, 2010.

INTERNET SITES

FactHound offers a safe, fun way to find Internet sites related to this book. All of the sites on FactHound have been researched by our staff.

Here's all you do:

Visit *www.facthound.com*

Type in this code: 9781491479827

Check out projects, games and lots more at
www.capstonekids.com

23

CRITICAL THINKING USING THE COMMON CORE

1. Why is it important for Bernese mountain dogs to be well trained?
   (Key Ideas and Details)

2. Would a Bernese mountain dog be a good city pet?
   Why or why not?
   (Integration of Knowledge and Ideas)

INDEX